Anything but Rover

Anything but Rover

THE ART AND SCIENCE OF NAMING YOUR DOG:

A Breed by Breed Guide, Including Mongrels

PETER MAYLE
Illustrated by Arthur Robins

ARTHUR BARKER LIMITED LONDON
A subsidiary of Weidenfeld (Publishers) Limited

Published in Great Britain by
Arthur Barker Limited
91 Clapham High Street
London SW4 7TA

ISBN 0 213 16928 2

Printed in Great Britain by
Butler & Tanner Ltd
Frome and London

In Memory of

ALFIE and RAINBOW and ZAPPA

Three dogs of uncertain
parentage who
triumphed over lack of
breeding to become
legends in their own
time and other people's
gardens.

INTRODUCTION

Forty million years ago, a distant relative of today's dog roamed the face of the earth. He was called Cynodictis. Not a snappy name, admittedly. Not the sort of name you or I might choose, perhaps, but quite harmless. Hardly a matter of life and death.

Alas, that's exactly what it turned out to be. Primitive man – particularly after a good lunch or when fuddled by sucking manioc root – found the name too much of a mouthful. It was a barrier to friendship. Then as now, it can be very difficult to establish a meaningful relationship with someone you can't pronounce.

Man and Cynodictis never did get on speaking terms, with the result that Cynodictis became extinct. He was eventually replaced by another creature – no stronger, no braver, no more intelligent, no more loyal and true, but destined for survival nevertheless. And all because of his name.

It was Canis.

Bearing in mind the limited vocal abilities of the time, Canis was an inspired choice. It was short, and easy to remember. More important, it was easy to say. Small cave-children could manage it within weeks of learning to grunt. And as history shows, the friendship between man and dog has flourished ever since.

You would think we'd have learned by now how important a name can be. But even today – when the winner of Cruft's is on *News at Ten*, when soaring achievements such as the bone-shaped biscuit are taken for granted, when the choice of

names is infinitely greater than it was a few million years ago
– even today, there are thousands of dogs who cringe every
time their names are called.

They put their paws over their ears, and affect deafness. They
find that they have urgent business elsewhere. They pretend to
be asleep. They cultivate an air of surprise – 'Are you talking
to *me?*' – to hide their self-consciousness. They hope their
friends aren't listening. They feel at a distinct social disadvantage. *And all because of their names.*

Ridiculous names. Names that cannot deliver the goods.
Names that make a dog feel like an Italian handbag or a
second-rate operetta. Names that lead to psychiatric disorders,
identity crises, loss of appetite, distemper, vicious attacks on
the furniture, flatulence and hardpad. It is difficult to exaggerate the effect that a poorly chosen name can have.

Mind you, it's far from easy to find what the French call the
nom juste. Should the choice be based on the dog's shape, his
colour and markings, his ethnic background, his family attributes, his personality and general disposition, the size of his
feet, the length of his tail, or what? This is complicated still
further by the fact that the name has to be chosen while the
dog is still too young to make his proclivities clear. His character is unformed, his eventual size often a mystery. You see? It's
tricky. And one must not forget that there's no such thing as
change of name by deed poll in the canine world. If he starts
out as Snuffles, the poor brute will have to slink through the
rest of his life as Snuffles.

Fortunately, as we shall see, there are some names which are
a perfect fit for certain dogs. But first, some general principles
which have been established over the years, and which no
sensible owner will ignore.

NAMES TO AVOID

The over-popular name

While walking her dog in Kensington Gardens, a woman stopped to chat to a friend. Her dog went off to amuse himself in the bushes, and when she looked round, he was nowhere to be seen. 'Henry!' she bellowed, 'come here at once!' Within seconds, fourteen assorted dogs called Henry (this was Kensington, remember) were milling round, as well as a passing stockbroker who thought his luck had changed.

This is all very well if you want company on your walks, or someone else's dog or husband following you home. If not, think twice about picking a name that's on everybody else's lips.

The scholarly name

Most often found in university towns, where owners like to display their academic backgrounds. Take a stroll through Oxford and you will invariably come across dogs with names like Agamemnon or Socrates or Homer. Highly amusing to the owner, of course, but not much fun for the dog who doesn't have a classical education, and who would rather be dealing with a lamp post than a series of iambic pentameters. In extreme cases, the scholarly name can lead to severe feelings of inferiority and a tendency to bite anybody wearing a gown, smoking a pipe, or belonging to the N.U.T.

The topical name

You meet them everywhere. Dogs named after characters in television series and films, dogs named after cabinet ministers, trade union leaders, sports personalities, newsreaders, astronauts, train robbers – anyone who is in the headlines for more than a week or two is commemorated all over the country by four-legged memorials. How many dogs do you think are called JR or Jaws or Tebbitt or Biggsy? Thousands? Hundreds of thousands? The trouble is that when the limelight passes on, the wretched dog is left with an out-of-date name and a lot of explaining to do to his younger friends.

First dog: 'Lucan? What kind of name is that?'
Second dog: 'Well, he was famous for disappearing, like me.'
First dog: 'Damn silly name.'

And so on. Nothing makes a dog feel more old-fashioned than a name whose fleeting moment of fame has passed.

The socially dangerous name

Here we tread on delicate ground indeed. Dozens of names that seem quite innocent in one part of the country can take on offensive connotations elsewhere. For example, one black Labrador we know has to use an alias whenever he visits London. His real name is quite acceptable in Leicestershire, but to mention it in Notting Hill is to risk an appearance in front of the Race Relations Board. Other areas to keep away from include homosexuality, football and the Royal Family, or a combination of all three.

The intimate name

Far be it from us to spoil those precious moments of almost mystical unity between you and your dog. All we would beg you to remember is this: the name that can be whispered in the privacy of the dog basket is not always appropriate in more public places. There you are, let's say, enjoying a walk with your dog in the park. All of a sudden, his attention is caught by one of those rather smart designer dogs like an Afghan. They circle each other, then bound off together. Isn't nature wonderful! The instant companionship of two healthy, fun-loving animals. However, a few moments later, you come to a small knot of people – two nuns, a police constable, and the Afghan's owner – who are watching in horror as your dog energetically pursues his ambition to make the Afghan the mother of his pups.

This is bad enough when your dog is called Bob or Spot. It is much, much worse when his name is one of those endearments which should never be uttered above a whisper. But you stand there, obliged to bawl it out at the top of your voice while the nuns have hysterics and the policeman can hardly take down your name and address for laughing. You blame the dog, of course, which is unfair. It's you who picked the name.

The upwardly mobile name

Embarrassment is not confined to dog owners. Dogs can suffer too.

A great friend of ours is an Airedale called Roy. His pedigree name is Beauregard of Caversham, and his owner, an Olympic-standard social climber, has the habit of calling him Beauregard in front of important guests to draw attention to his noble breeding. The dog, an unpretentious soul, finds this so embarrassing that he flattens his ears and hides in the garage every time it happens. There he stays until sanity returns and he is allowed to be Roy again. Dogs know when you're laughing at them.

There is one other potentially disastrous way to pick a dog's name, and that is to let a child do it. Would you let a dog pick your child's name? Of course not. Certain matters are best left to mature and intelligent people like yourself.

*   *   *   *   *

EQUAL RIGHTS FOR BITCHES

Out of courtesy, and to avoid being attacked and possibly bitten by the militant feminist dog lobby, we would like to acknowledge the special problems that accompany the naming of a bitch.

Not only do we have to consider size, shape, colouring and quirks of character; there is also the most intimate personal characteristic of all – sex – to take into account. Instantly, we are faced with a string of dilemmas:

Should gender be allowed to dominate the choice of name (i.e. Alice), or should the more general principle of matching the name to a distinctive facet of personality (i.e. Stinker) be followed?

Will the choice of a bi-sexual name affect the maternal urge? Would a bitch called Digger ever feel sufficiently feminine to procreate? And if so, what in God's name would she produce? Australian Terriers? Moles?

Should we allow the Government to get away with its blatantly sexist demands for 37½ pence for a dog licence, or should we make a stand and insist on a bitch licence? Or again, should we lie low and pretend we've got a dog? But if we do, what happens when the dog licence detector van comes round? How are we going to explain away an officially masculine creature called Vera?

What allowances should be made for the future growth of facial hair? Many breeds do not develop a full set of whiskers until early adulthood, and there's the problem. You choose a romantic and feminine name for your smooth-cheeked puppy, she grows up, and you find yourself harbouring a bearded lady with a moustache that could put a broom to shame. And she's called Chloe. Result: unkind laughter from your friends, and yet another self-conscious dog.

There are no easy answers. Your best bet is to choose a sturdy, no-nonsense feminine name such as Hilda or Minnie. Far better a plain name for a glamorous bitch than the other way round.

*   *   *   *   *

HOW WOULD *YOU* LIKE TO
BE CALLED ROVER?

Pedigree dogs, with their own private family trees and certificates of ancestry as long as your leg, do not take kindly to the standard all-purpose name. It's not that they're snobs necessarily, but one can see their point: is it right that the result of generations of careful breeding ends up with a name like Fido? How can a potential Best of Breed at Cruft's hold his head up when everyone knows that his intimates call him Rover?

A wise and sensitive owner bears this in mind, and takes the time to select a name appropriate to the breed. As far as we know, this aspect of naming dogs has never been officially documented, so the guide that follows is something of a breakthrough. Unfortunately, it is incomplete. There are more than three hundred internationally recognised breeds, and we can't deal with them all here. But we've made a brave start. On the following pages, you will find personality notes and naming suggestions for some of the most popular breeds in the country, with a separate section devoted to that most popular breed of all, the mongrel.

*　　*　　*　　*　　*

THE BASSET HOUND

Canis lugubriensis

A most deceptive hound, the Basset. To look at his face you would think that he alone was responsible for dealing with the worries of the world. What is behind that mournful expression? Concerns about inflation and unemployment? Misgivings about the arms limitation talks? Apprehension about the ozone layer?

Not a bit of it. Behind that doleful countenance is a cheerful

and jaunty personality. He is, in the old-fashioned sense, a gay dog. He loves a romp.

The misleading appearance, of course, is caused by some confusion many generations ago in the outerwear department. The Basset was issued with a larger dog's coat, presumably on the assumption that he would grow into it. He didn't, as one can plainly see. The skin falls over the eyes, the coat is baggy, the socks are wrinkled, the effect generally is one of sartorial disarray, not helped by the occasional black toenail among the white ones. Despite this, or perhaps because of it, you can't help smiling when you see a Basset Hound. And somewhere under all those wrinkles you can be sure he's smiling back.

Recommended names

Dignified but slightly unusual names can help to bring out the real hound: Abner, Gascoigne, Eloise, Brinsley, etc. You might also find inspiration in the Yellow Pages if you look at the listing for Antique Dealers.

Names to avoid

Anything to do with short legs, crumpled complexions or Hush Puppies.

THE DACHSHUND

Canis under Alles

There are six distinct types of Dachshund. The lowest of the low is the *Zwergteckel*, or Dwarf Dachshund, who holds the unofficial record for the stumpiest legs in the business. He is undismayed. He knows that mere length of limb is much less important than size of personality, and nobody could accuse a Dachshund of having an undersized personality.

If you compare their profiles, you will notice a passing similarity between the Dachshund and the Doberman, and it's easy to imagine the wistful Dachshund sitting there and thinking to himself: 'There but for another eighteen inches of leg go I.' It is at moments like this that breeding comes through. Is he envious? Does he brood? Do his whiskers droop with melancholy? Never!

With a fine display of positive thinking, off he goes to intimidate the first large dog he can find, not through superior combat techniques or a faster bite, but through sheer force of ego. You can't help admiring his effrontery, and he knows it. With a final growl he will leave his victim and return to you, demonstrating *en route* that it is possible to swagger even though your undercarriage is barely three inches from the ground.

Recommended names

All male Dachshunds would secretly like to be called Frederick the Great, but they will make do with the name of any reasonably successful Emperor or Royal Personage. The female is more modest in her preferences, but still requires to be treated with a certain dignity; Mitzi is about as informal as she cares to go.

Names to avoid

Wiener Schnitzel, Liverwurst, Chipolata or any other species of sausage.

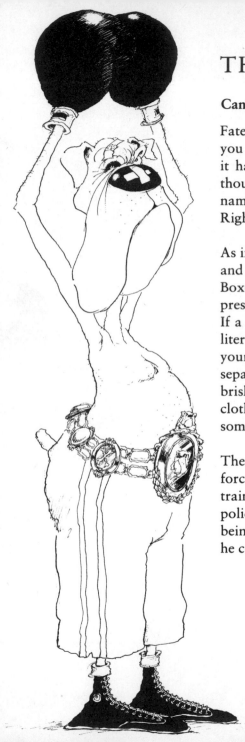

THE BOXER

Canis Pugilisticus

Fate can deal some unkind blows. If you had a face that looked as though it had been on the receiving end of a thousand straight lefts, what family name would you least like to have? Right first time: Boxer.

As if to make up for his battered profile and welterweight appearance, the Boxer has a charming nature, often expressed in a flatteringly damp fashion. If a Boxer likes you, he marinates you, literally salivating with pleasure at your company. When at last you are separated by the referee, you'll need a brisk rubdown and a change into dry clothes, but it's nice to know that someone appreciates you.

There are, so we're told, several police forces round the world who have trained Boxers to become skilled in police work, the dog's only bad habit being a tendency to shake hands before he comes out biting.

Recommended names

Heroes of the ring – Dempsey, Sugar Ray, Marvellous Marvin – are useful sources of inspiration for male dogs. For the Boxer bitch, the more old-fashioned names can be surprisingly successful. We once knew two Boxer sisters who were very well suited with the names Ernestine and Mildred.

Names to avoid

References to the generous flow of saliva or the breed's characteristically heavy breathing – the Dribbles and Sniffles group of names – are out. So is Rocky, although Sylvester is just possible.

THE DOBERMAN

Canis Schnappshund von Thuringia

Some time during the middle of the nineteenth century, there lived in Germany a bailiff with a nervous disposition. His name was Doberman.

Doberman's job, which consisted mainly of persuading people to pay up on old debts, frequently exposed him to abuse and the risk of attack. This made his nervous disposition even more nervous but, so modest were bailiffs' wages in those days, he couldn't afford a minder. He decided to breed his own protection. Hence the bailiff's dog, or, as it soon came to be called, the Doberman.

The Doberman is the ideal companion for anyone in a hazardous line of work – fearless, devoted to its master or mistress, and ready to savage the enemy at the first hint of a command. As a Doberman owner, you need to be very careful indeed about making sudden noises. An aggressive-sounding cough, a carelessly aimed grunt, even a muffled sneeze can easily be misinterpreted as the signal to kill. It's no good telling the victim afterwards that it was all a terrible mistake. A Doberman's bite is infinitely worse than his bark.

Recommended names

Nobody would dare to laugh at whatever you call a Doberman, so you can indulge in flights of fancy if you feel like it. Names taken from the Prussian aristocracy (Bismarck), from the armed forces (Rommel), or from primitive mythology (Beowulf) have the right flavour. Gengis is also a popular choice.

Names to avoid

Cuddly or facetious names make a Doberman uncomfortable. Don't chance it.

THE CORGI

Canis Cardigan and Canis Pembroke

The Cardigan side of the Corgi family has the longer tail. The Pembroke side has the baggier trousers. Apart from that, they are very similar, so we shall treat them as one breed.

The clue to the Corgi's character is his height; or rather, his lack of it. Just as it does in the case of short men, lack of stature exerts a tremendous influence on bearing, behaviour and lust for power. (History is full of examples, such as Alexander the Great, Napoleon, Michael Jackson, and many others.) In order to compensate for his shortness of leg and uncomfortable proximity to the ground, the Corgi has developed several distinctive characteristics.

First, he is very rarely seen without his ears fully extended upwards. This is often mistaken for alertness, but in fact it is an ingenious attempt to appear taller. Since a Corgi's ears are almost as long as his legs, you can see that a cocked ear makes a big difference.

Along with the upright ears, the Corgi has cultivated an impressively business-like air. He is never idle, but always *en route* from one appointment to the next. When confined to one place for any length of time, he fidgets. If he were an executive, he'd always be looking at his watch and making telephone calls. It's all part of the need to be perceived as *someone of importance.*

And this is where his size becomes a distinct advantage. As dogs go, the Corgi is very easy to pack. He fits comfortably under a plane seat, next to the chauffeur in a limousine, or in the luggage rack of the Royal train to Balmoral. He thus qualifies as hand baggage, and can travel with the family. Most important, he can be photographed disembarking with the family. At these moments, you will notice that his ears are so strenuously cocked that they threaten to leave his head.

Recommended names

Dylan, Myfanwy, Blodwen, Dai – the shorter Welsh names are very appropriate. Quick, efficient names – Tom, Dick, Harry, Di – are also good, as are names that imply status and executive potency: Memo, Reagan, Downing, Chief Whip, Visa, etc.

Names to avoid

The longer Welsh names, since they are often longer than the dog itself, are not advisable. Nor are Welsh surnames, no matter how amusing they may seem at first. Corgis called Rhys-Jones or Evans-The-Post quickly tire of the inevitable ethnic remarks which accompany the name, and take their revenge under the dinner table. Many a Corgi-baiter has suffered frayed ankles as a result of an ill-considered Welsh joke.

THE OLD ENGLISH SHEEPDOG

Canis Bobtail domesticus

This breed narrowly escapes the fate of the Puli, which looks the same at both ends, and is always having titbits and endearments proffered to an unreceptive backside. Fortunately for the Old English Sheepdog, he has a highly polished and visible nose which makes it easy to recognise the conversational end.

But there's more to the Old English Sheepdog than a useful nose. This is the only dog to have if you've always wanted a bear but have never had the private frozen lake and three hundred acres of tundra to put it in. Our theory, which is regarded with horror by the Kennel Club, is that the Old English is in fact *descended* from bears. Canine experts can go on about its similarities to the Russian Owtchar or the Italian Bergamese until they're blue in the face, but we know bear-like traits when we see them. There are three characteristics in particular which prove our point.

The Walk	Get down on your hands and knees and watch a polar bear walk towards you. Notice the swinging motion. Now do the same thing with an Old English Sheepdog. The walks are *identical*.
The Arctic Roll	There is nothing an Old English Sheepdog likes more than a long and thorough roll in deep snow. Again, one only has to observe the polar bear in mid-roll to see the uncanny family resemblance.

Preferred Diet	The Old English Sheepdog is *very* fond of honey. What other animal can you think of with the same weakness? Exactly.

Recommended names

Plain homespun names like George and Martha and Percy suit the breed best. It is, after all, an English country dog and should have a name to match. Winnie is good for either sex.

Names to avoid

Whimsical urban names (Battersea, Indiana Bones, etc.) are a mistake. And for God's sake don't even think of calling the poor beast Dulux.

THE GREAT DANE

Canis Gigantissimus

Why these dogs should be called Great Danes when they have no connection with Denmark is a mystery. This is just one of many reasons for the puzzled air which causes a semi-permanent furrow in the Great Dane brow.

In fact, almost every aspect of life is faintly puzzling if you happen to be several sizes too big for your surroundings. The right setting for a Great Dane is a baronial hall, where there's room enough to wag the tail without causing structural damage. Sadly, baronial halls are few and far between, so most Great Danes are obliged to spend their lives trying to fold themselves into small rooms, small cars or small armchairs. No wonder they look puzzled.

Then there is the sometimes ticklish business of smaller beings walking up and down underneath them. Cats, other dogs, children, the occasional short adult – the flow of traffic through a Great Dane's legs is often heavy and sometimes congested. How would you feel if you had a cat and an eighteen-month-old child exchanging insults just beneath your stomach? Uneasy, no doubt. But this is the kind of situation Great Danes have to put up with all the time.

All the more remarkable, really, that they are such gentle and good-natured dogs. Immune from claustrophobia, patient and loyal, they ask little more from life than that you walk round them instead of under them.

Recommended names

Noble names with classical origins are good for either sex:

Brutus, Juno, Achilles, Dido, Eurydice, Hector. A quick glance through Homer will give you a dozen ideas.

Names to avoid

Lofty. Shorty. Anything Danish, like Carlsberg or Victor Borge. Anything too jocular. Great Danes have enough to put up with already.

THE JACK RUSSELL TERRIER

Canis Reverendii

Everyone knows that the St Bernard is one dog who has close ties, through the monks, with Mother Church: few people know that the Jack Russell is another.

The breed was more or less invented by Parson Jack Russell in the heyday of the sporting clergyman. Country vicars were

expected to ride to hounds, shoot straight and keep the crypt and the vicarage free from rats. This, presumably, is what prompted Parson Jack to take up terrier breeding, because the Jack Russell is a ferociously effective ratter. But not only rats. Foxes, rabbits, squirrels, the boy who delivers the newspapers – virtually any moving object which offers the chance of a sporting encounter will do.

Curiously enough for such a popular breed, the Jack Russell is not officially recognised by many canine organisations, and the effects of this snub show in personality compensation.

Depending on whether or not you are an admirer of the breed, the Jack Russell character can either be described as forceful and self-confident, or overbearing and tiresome. However you describe it, you cannot ignore it: Jack Russells have presence. Unfortunately, it is this very quality combined with the accident of their initials that started the epidemic of terriers called JR. We can only hope that it will go the way of other afflictions like the Bubonic Plague and disappear.

Recommended names

Traditionalists favour names like Jack The Nipper, Russell, Toby and Punch. Rev (or Reverend on Sundays) is often found in hunting country. In other words, short, brisk names are preferred. Those of you who lean towards languorous or romantic names should stick to less energetic breeds.

Names to avoid

Complicated or pretentious names like Stanislaus or Algernon or Genevieve simply add to the Jack Russell's already strong feelings of self-importance and will only lead to demands for a larger basket and a personal kennel-maid.

THE PEKINESE

Canis Inscrutabilis

You may think, as we once did, that this is just another breed of dog. Slightly squatter than most, maybe, and with more exotic uncles and aunts, but a dog nevertheless. How wrong we were.

According to Chinese legend, the Pekinese is the result of a most unlikely union between a lion and a she-monkey. Those of us with a practical turn of mind can immediately see difficulties in this arrangement, but the Chinese tell us that the god Hai Ho sorted everything out, and thus the Pekinese was born.

Curiously enough, there *is* a definite leonine side to his character. Anyone who has seen a Pekinese defending his territory against a pair of strange and threatening ankles will have noticed his spirit, his courage, and a self-confidence out of all proportion to his killing power. And there, in a nutshell, is the essence of the Pekinese: he genuinely believes himself to be a large dog. The fact that he can actually walk underneath a Great Dane with at least two feet of clearance to spare doesn't alter his conviction that he's up there with the big breeds.

Bear this in mind when choosing a name. As Confucius was so fond of saying, 'Peke with silly name takes revenge on curtains'.

Recommended names

Sonorous, gong-like names are always suitable, specially when they also refer to an ancient Chinese dynasty. Ming is the classic example. T'ang is also good. Wong, on the other hand, is not. No dog wants to sound like a Chinese laundry.

Names to avoid

Diminutive names, like Puffles and Snooky and anything ending in '-kins' will be treated with the contempt they deserve or ignored altogether. Any name that suits a small dog is wrong, since a Pekinese will always think you're talking to somebody else.

THE POODLE

Canis Sapiens

If ever a dog suffered from bad luck, it is the Poodle.

The name itself is frivolous and slightly silly. The same can be said of many owners, who seem to compete with each other in terms of wretched excess. Thus we find Poodles dyed pink, Poodles with scarlet lacquer and glitterdust toenails, Poodles with matching bootees and coatees, Poodles clipped until they resemble absurd pieces of mobile topiary, Poodles with their own beauty parlours, their own health farms, their own psychiatrists, their own nervous disorders and skin complaints – in other words, they are treated like freaks until inevitably they become freaks.

And yet this is one of the cleverest breeds of all. The most highly skilled performing-dog acts are nearly always Poodles, and their capacity for learning is extraordinary. They are sensitive and intelligent creatures, and this is the worst piece of luck of all. A dumb dog wouldn't mind being dressed in a turquoise fun-fur walking ensemble, but Poodles are bright enough to be mortified with embarrassment. Can you blame them for yapping?

Recommended names

A Poodle will be eternally grateful for a normal name: Curly, Sooty, Kafka, Sid. Give him an ordinary name and an ordinary haircut and you'll have a friend for life.

Names to avoid

The double-barrelled Gallic names, like Jean-Claude or Marie-Louise, have been overdone. The Finchley Road boutique type of name (anything ending in -ucci, -icci, -acci) is best left to boutiques. Mimi, Tutu, Zizi and Frou-Frou are merely the first steps on the road that leads to painted toenails and diamanté collars. Ugh.

THE ALSATIAN

Canis Deutscher Schaferhund

The canine equivalent of the SAS – brave, fierce, capable of leaping small buildings at a single bound, and more than a match for any postman – this is not a dog to be trifled with.

As you might expect when you consider his German ancestry, the Alsatian is not famous for his frivolous nature and irrepressible sense of humour. He is a serious dog, at his happiest, like most Germans, when he's working. Give him something to guard or, as a special treat, dress up as a policeman when you take him out for a walk. Alsatians love uniforms, because they feel they're out on security patrol work. However, they do enjoy some playful moments. If you have an obliging friend who likes a bit of rough-and-tumble, give him a thirty-second start and then set the dog on him. You will find that your Alsatian will soon enter into the spirit of things, and it won't be long before bringing down running human figures takes over from fetching the stick as his favourite game.

All in all, a good dog to have on your side.

Recommended names

Anything with a military flavour, so long as it's over the rank of Corporal. Sensible Teutonic names, such as Wagner, Siegfried or Max. Brisk and descriptive names, like Wolf, Fang and Attila. Aristocratic titles – Queenie, Prince, etc. – are pretentious but acceptable.

Names to avoid

The German joke names: Fritzi, Putzi, Adolf and Himmler (funnily enough, Himmler is perfectly acceptable for a Dachs-

hund – probably something to do with the shortness of leg).
Names that sound too much like commands are risky; they are
easily mistaken for signals to attack, as in 'Rolf! Rolf! Oh my
God, I'm terribly sorry. I'll go and call an ambulance.' Effeminate names are out, even for bitches. Sheba is just about OK.
Irma and Gertie are not.

THE SCOTTISH TERRIER

Canis McCanis

Back in the days before television and organised football, the
way to spend a Saturday afternoon was to go burrow hunting.
The idea was simple enough (dog goes in one end of burrow,
and startled local resident pops out of the other end), but the
difficulty was always to find the right dog, both in size and
temperament. Small dogs were often too timid; brave dogs
often too big. It took a breeder in Aberdeen to come up with
the perfect combination.

The Scottish Terrier has everything one could possibly need to
go down a burrow. His compact size and powerful dorsal
muscles allow him to get up a good turn of speed underground.
His keen sense of smell guides him through the one-way system. His huge and intimidating eyebrows protect his eyes, and
his surprisingly large teeth protect the rest of him. It would
take a desperate fox indeed to face up to all that.

Above ground, he is lively and sociable. He will endure jokes about sporrans and whisky. He will even tolerate the inevitable comparison between his eyebrows and Denis Healey's. It is when people nudge him and say 'Och aye' and 'Hoots' that his patience runs out and he turns nasty.

Recommended names

They may be clichés, but Jock, Aggie, Hamish, Dougal, McGillicuddy of the Reeks and other Scottish names are still worth considering.

Names to avoid

Paddy.

THE AFGHAN HOUND

Canis Bouffant

There are several breeds which, through no fault of their own, have become fashion accessories first and dogs second. The Afghan is one of them.

You see Afghans walking rather self-consciously down the street, attached by a lead to a girl with the same hairstyle. You see them looking supercilious in the back of expensive cars. You see them looking bored in advertisements for socially ambitious clothes.

It's a great shame. The Afghan is a superb hunting dog, a 'sight hound' who uses his eyes rather than his sense of smell to find his quarry, and his amazing turn of speed to run it down. Watch an Afghan in a park going after a smaller dog or a short woman in a fur coat (their eyesight is keen, but they do make the occasional mistake), and you will marvel at the efficient way in which they seize their prey and wrestle it to the ground. Not surprisingly, this kind of incident has given the Afghan a reputation for unreliable and anti-social behaviour. But what can you expect? If you restrict a hunting dog to pavements, cars and photographic studios, it's bound to go bananas occasionally. Blood will out.

Recommended names

Names connoting speed are very good. So are names that hark (or maybe bark) back to the Afghan's exotic Eastern ancestry. You could always combine the two, as in Flash Ali. Garbo is also good.

Names to avoid

Ordinary names will just encourage further bad behaviour. Call an Afghan Bert and you're asking for trouble.

THE MONGREL

Canis Vulgaris

There are, so we're told, more than six million dogs in Britain. Probably half of them are mongrels. To a serious student of canine matters, this is the most fascinating and scientifically rewarding breed of all. It comes in every conceivable shape, size, colour and inside leg measurement, and offers the adventurous owner a chance to acquire something unique in the animal kingdom: a genuine prototype.

This happened to some friends of ours recently, who had the good fortune to be presented with the first examples of what could be a *completely new breed*. It came about, as these things sometimes do in romantic novels, on holiday. During a chance encounter in the boarding kennels, a young Dalmatian bitch succumbed to the experienced wiles of an agile Corgi. She returned home 'in pup'. The Dalmatian's owners, being pedigree snobs, were horrified. As soon as was decently possible they gave the offspring away. Our friends were the recipients.

It's still early days. They won't know for another few months whether the pups will grow up to be spotted Corgis, or Dalmatians with compressed legs and furry gaiters, or some even more startling mixture of the two breeds. But that's the magic of the mongrel. You don't just get a pup. You get a surprise as well.

This obviously complicates the business of selecting a suitable name. As a simple example, take the question of size. With a pedigree breed, you can forecast to within an inch or two how big the adult dog will be. The size of a mongrel, with its father not available for comment and its ancestry a matter of conjecture, is at best a wild supposition. All you can do is take a close look at the paws. If they seem unnaturally large for one so young, there is a possibility that the fully-grown dog will be unnaturally large too. On the other hand, with the typical unpredictability of the breed, it might just end up as a small dog with big feet. Who can tell? The prudent owner, therefore, will avoid any name that makes a specific reference to size.

Oddly enough, although the physical size and shape of the mongrel are difficult to establish in advance, there are several other attributes that are sufficiently widespread and well defined to be considered part of the mongrel ethos. It is in the hope that these attributes will inspire you to great feats of name-calling that we list them here.

Personality

Mongrels have the shameless persistence of encyclopaedia salesmen. They may want food. They may want sticks to be thrown. They may want the bitch next door. They may want to sit in the passenger seat of the car instead of in the boot. They may want to jump on to a particularly delicate and expensive piece of furniture, or on to an old and favoured relative. What they want may vary, but how they get what they want is by using standard mongrel tactics: (A) the soulful gaze, (B) crude flattery, (C) threatening to be sick, (D) being sick. One of these always works.

Feeding habits

Mongrels will eat anything put in front of them (and sometimes anything that is put on the table just above them), but they prefer food that is not intended for them. Their idea of heaven is to be let loose on the rich remains of a dinner party for eight: a little smoked salmon mousse, a mouthful or two of breast of chicken in cream and cognac sauce, some nicely rotting Stilton, followed by profiteroles, followed by acute diarrhoea. This is not mere greed, but gastronomic pessimism. Mongrels feel that every meal may be their last, and stuff themselves accordingly.

Breeding habits

Mongrels like sex. If other dogs aren't available, they will form
passionate liaisons with cushions, little Sally's teddy bear, the
vicar's leg, or the bottom of your rich uncle's astrakhan over-
coat. They are relentless in their search for love, and will travel
many miles for the sake of a fleeting assignation. Male mongrels are known to be extremely potent, and females very fer-
tile. Litters of seventeen are not uncommon.

Escapist tendencies

Mongrels are not easily restrained. They, alone among dogs,
have been known to chew chains. They can slip a collar that
is almost tight enough for strangulation. Fences too high to be

jumped are burrowed under. Ropes and leather leads are gnawed to pieces. The tiniest apertures are somehow squeezed through. They are the Houdinis of the dog world, and their urge to escape is not always prompted by thoughts of food or sex; it's freedom they love. (If that happens to include food and sex, so much the better, but the main thing is to wander at will.)

Social graces

Mongrels are socially dangerous, since they thrive on embarrassment. They can be guaranteed to growl at your dearest friends and fraternise with undesirable people trying to sell you magazine subscriptions. If you should have a few neighbours round one evening, your mongrel will be found asleep on someone's fur coat. Other favourite party tricks include knocking over drinks with their tails, startling female guests by applying a cold nose up the skirt from behind, eating the carelessly placed pipe or bunch of car keys, and barking hysterically outside the lavatory door whenever the lavatory is in use. There is only one visitor who is assured of a warm, quiet welcome, and that is the thief in the night. Mongrels adore

burglars, probably because they feel some kind of affinity with them. Social outcasts stick together.

Genetic certainties

1. Mongrels will give birth at the most inconvenient time.
2. The bad habits of both parents will be combined and magnified in the young.

Recommended names

Your guess is as good as ours.

Names to avoid

Anything remotely aristocratic. While it is true that many mongrels have a high opinion of themselves, they do not feel at ease with pretension. In fact, one of their small pleasures is to jeer at any dog with a *nouveau pedigree* name.

THE BULL TERRIER

Canis Dens Colossus Hinkiensis

This is one of the few dogs to have been deliberately bred as an offensive weapon, and should therefore be treated with some caution. This is not to say the Bull Terrier has a vicious temperament. As a rule, it is docile and good-natured, ready to pass the time of day with other dogs and, after a couple of amiable sniffs, move on. The trouble, and there frequently *is* trouble, is invariably started by the other dog.

It is the Local-Hero-Meets-Famous-Boxer-in-Pub syndrome. There is always someone who thinks he can beat the champ. In the case of the Bull Terrier, it is wishful thinking. Other dogs, no matter how large, should remember that the Bull Terrier was originally bred to fight bulls. The jaws are big enough to fasten on a bull's muzzle, and the average time it takes to unclamp those jaws is forty-five minutes. There is the famous story of a Bull Terrier who dragged home a full-sized

mahogany chest of drawers from a junk yard, a distance of over a mile. Can you imagine any ordinary dog being able to do that? Or indeed, any ordinary removal man?

Attached to those imposing jaws you will find a most engaging character: a dog with a sense of humour and the distinctive, rolling walk of a sailor on shore leave looking for the nearest pub. James Hinks, the famous breeder who introduced the modern Bull Terrier, can rest content in his grave.

Recommended names

Anything resembling a short uppercut – Jack, Butch, Champ, Snap, Sykes, etc. – will do very well for a male dog. For a bitch, the homelier names are somehow best: Vera, Alice, Florrie, Rose. If you want to pay a small tribute to the breeder, Hinks isn't a bad choice either.

Names to avoid

Flowery or elegant names do not suit either sex. Gaylord, Antoinette, Hermione or Dorian do not sit comfortably with a shark-sized mouth and a physique like a Japanese wrestler.

THE SPANIEL

Canis Cocker (G.B.)

The Spaniel family is almost as numerous and widely spread as the Italian Royal family, and it's important to specify the type required when placing your order. Spaniels can be anything from a King Charles (small, slightly pop-eyed and often found in boudoirs) to an American (flared trouser bottoms and a heavily accented bark). Then there's the Clumber, the Field, the Irish Water, the Springer, the Sussex, and others. All spaniels, and all different.

The spaniel's spaniel, however, the type that many people regard as the classic example of the breed, is the genuine Cocker.

The Cocker is faithful, intelligent, and desperately eager to be of service. Here is a dog that really will go and fetch your slippers. As a hunting dog, he would prefer that you shot them first, but if that would cause too many problems with the neighbours a canine version of Hunt the Slipper is the next best thing. Search and retrieval are meat and drink to Cockers, and a well-hidden slipper will keep them happily occupied for hours.

As for names, you will find that the Cocker is not proud; he will come even when sworn at, so anxious is he to join in and be considered one of the family. Perhaps his only serious drawback shows itself at mealtimes. The combination of a voracious appetite and king-size ears can lead to some painful moments when the ear, lightly seasoned after being dipped in the food, is mistaken for the final mouthful. This accounts for the slightly frayed ears in young and inexperienced dogs, and the hideous practice of tying the poor brute's ears above his head before dinner, making him look (and probably feel) exactly like a woman caught in her curlers.

Recommended names

Anything you would call your butler will do very well, as it will reflect a certain dignified servility. Higgins, Jackson, Jenkins – straightforward, no-nonsense, honest British names. Or you can try for a name that captures the search and retrieval aspects of your dog's character, such as Hoover. Or you can just shout. He'll come.

Names to avoid

Cheap shots about length of ear, size of appetite, willingness to roll over on the back and have the stomach tickled, or any derivations of the word 'Cocker'.

THE LABRADOR

Canis Fetchit

The Labrador is possibly the most assiduous retriever of them all, and life and the daily round for a Labrador owner are full of surprises. What other dog, without a word of encouragement from you, will deliver something different to your door every day? A discarded umbrella, an old shoe, a long-lost glove, a size 37B bra, the day before yesterday's *Financial Times*, a stick, a ruptured tennis ball, a dead vole – there is no end to the rich variety of small and unsought-for objects that will come your way.

This is tangible proof of the Labrador's powerful instinct to please. If there were any justice in the world, this breed would have been officially appointed to handle Public Relations for the Man's Best Friend movement years ago. Labradors are *wonderful* with people. They like postmen, they like milkmen, they like burglars. They love your friends. And the sight of a

new person makes a Labrador's tail spin round like the rotor-blade of a helicopter on heat. As if that weren't welcome enough, some precious relic is then exhumed from the compost heap and brought into the house for personal delivery to the guest. While it may look like a pile of putrefied owl droppings to you, to the Labrador it's a gift of love. What are a few square yards of ruined carpet compared with this kind of generosity?

Recommended names

The more you make a Labrador feel like a person, the happier it will be. It is a sturdy, middle-class breed, and enjoys names like Charlie, Susie, Henry and Emma. Surnames make it feel unloved.

Names to avoid

Nothing *too* jokey (they're easily hurt), and nothing you'd be ashamed to call out while rough shooting.

WHEN TWO NAMES ARE
WORSE THAN ONE

Finding the right name for one dog is, as we have seen, fraught with problems. Finding the right names for two dogs is

doubly fraught, and many owners panic into taking the easy option.

The easy option is to select the name of a commercial enterprise and apply it to your dogs. Over the years, we have known a Bulldog and a Spaniel called Fortnum and Mason, a Poodle and a Labrador called Justerini and Brooks, two identical Beagles called Saatchi and Saatchi – there's no doubt that linked names can be very effective.

There is, however, a tragic snag. Sooner or later, one half of the partnership will be called to the Great Kennel in the Sky, leaving you with one dog and half a pair of names. Of course, you get another dog. And, of course, the vacant name doesn't suit him. The result is what is known in naming circles as a flawed pair: Fortnum and Bonzo, or Justerini and Buster. Be warned.

IN PRAISE OF SHORT NAMES

In dog naming, as in every other highly specialised skill, we can learn from the professionals.

The professionals here are a mixed bunch. They are farmers, shepherds, Securicor guards, sniffer-dog handlers, poachers, and hairdressers with Bosnian Mastiff attack dogs. What they have in common is the need to communicate as quickly as possible with their dogs in any kind of weather, or in circumstances of acute emergency.

Almost without exception, they prefer the short name. Just one syllable, which can be hurled into the teeth of a Highland gale, which will carry halfway across Wimbledon Common, which will stop an enraged cat-owner in his tracks, which can

be heard above the roar of traffic or the bleating of sheep or the gusty sighs of a bitch in heat – just one syllable.

You won't find the pro walking around with a dog called Heseltine or Fortescue. Not for him the elaborate conceits of the amateur. His dog has a name that is somewhere between a belch and a short German preposition. Not pretty, perhaps, but eminently practical. (Incidentally, you will notice that even the commentator on *One Man and His Dog* is called Phil. Not Philip. Phil.)

One final tip: approximately 72% of all working male collies are called Bob, which makes it a one-syllable name to avoid.